■ □ ■ □ ■

A VOICE

Writings from an Unbound Europe

■ □ ■ □ ■

ANZHELINA POLONSKAYA

A VOICE

SELECTED POEMS

Edited and translated from the Russian
by Andrew Wachtel

NORTHWESTERN UNIVERSITY PRESS

EVANSTON, ILLINOIS

Northwestern University Press
Evanston, Illinois 60208-4170

Published 2004 by Northwestern University Press.
English translation and introduction copyright © 2004 by Andrew Wachtel.
Originally published in Russian in 2002 under the title *Golos*.
Copyright © 2002 by Anzhelina Polonskaya. All rights reserved.

Printed in the United States of America

10 9 8 7 6 5 4 3 2 1

ISBN 0-8101-2088-7 (CLOTH)
ISBN 0-8101-2089-5 (PAPER)

Library of Congress Cataloging-in-Publication data are available from
the Library of Congress.

The paper used in this publication meets the minimum requirements of the American
National Standard for Information Sciences—Permanence of Paper for Printed Library
Materials, ANSI Z39.48-1992.

■ □ ■ □ ■

CONTENTS

CODA

■ □ ■ □ ■

TRANSLATOR'S
INTRODUCTION

I was first introduced to the poetry of Anzhelina Polonskaya in 1999. We were organizing a poetry festival at Northwestern University that was to feature poets from three countries (Russia, Poland, and Slovenia) and from three generations. Having invited Andrei Voznesensky to take part as a member of the oldest generation, we asked him to recommend a poet of the youngest generation. He proposed Polonskaya, who had recently returned to Moscow from a two-year stint working as an ice dancer in Central and South America for a traveling Russian troupe.

When Polonskaya's poems arrived, I discovered that her background and subsequent career choice were not her only unusual features. The poems themselves were extremely surprising and revealed a unique and highly independent artistic voice. Unlike the majority of Russian poets, Polonskaya did not receive a classical literary education. Rather, her poetry comes almost exclusively out of her own experience and, even more important, out of her own thoughts. This is not to say that Polonskaya is uneducated. She has read widely in Russian (Brodsky, Tsvetaeva, Akhmatova, and Mayakovsky being particularly important), Anglo-American, and Spanish poetry. Nevertheless, her lack of literary education has allowed her to be far freer in her relationship with previous poets than are many of her contemporaries, who frequently seem to be engaged in a hermetically sealed dialogue with the tradition. Thus, while one can find echoes of the diction of other poets in her work, her poetry lacks the typical self-consciousness of those poets who are more immediately aware of the weight of literary tradition. Polonskaya consciously guards her outsider status, choosing to live not in Moscow itself but in the little town of Malakhovka, some thirty miles from the center of the city, a peaceful enclave far from the daily squabbles of Moscow literary life.

Polonskaya was born in Malakhovka in 1969. She published her first collection of poetry, *My Heavenly Torch,* in 1993. This collection was followed by a second book in 1998 entitled simply *Poems.* A third collection, *The Sky Through a Private's Eye,* was published in 1999, and her fourth and most recent collection, *A Voice,* appeared in 2002. The poems in this first English-language book-length collection are drawn from Polonskaya's two most recent books, but I have chosen not to present them chronologically. (As Polonskaya almost always dates her poems, however, the reader can re-create the chronology of the composition should he or she so desire.) Rather, the poems are grouped in three loose thematic sections entitled "Portraits," "Elegies," and "Times, Places, Moods" because I feel that grouping poems that in some way echo each other allows for a better appreciation of Polonskaya's talent.

The collection opens with the title poem, "A Voice." An examination of this poem is a good place to begin in order to appreciate Polonskaya's poetics.

A voice bouncing off boarded-up windows, a quivering voice
within walls like well-driven nails.
A throaty voice, as of a caged dove,
groping through deaf darkness into bunches of hanging fingers.

Through them, through the air heated by snow,
torn apart like fabric, like flesh that has known the scalpel.
How silent it is! Either a hot flash on the cheek
or simply snowflakes melting and rolling down like tears.

That voice! Free, unmaimed by wheels, not pursued,
edgy, floating beneath the damp stone vaults,
remarked only by the lightning glances of parishioners
who will remain in this blue twilight, today or tomorrow.

Like so many of Polonskaya's poems, this one presents, in extremely terse and condensed form, a mysterious narrative. Through the point of view of a watchful, sympathetic, yet just slightly ironic voice, we see a scene that burns itself into our consciousness while remaining eerie. A number of thematic concerns that reappear frequently in Polonskaya's poetry are apparent here: a fascination with desolate places, with a complex synesthesia of sound, sight, touch, and smell, and the omnipresence of maimed bodies and death. Polonskaya's favorite tropes are here as well: complex, original extended metaphors and ellipses (in this and in much else, her poetry clearly builds on the tradition of Marina Tsvetaeva). The frequent presence of ellipses in her work makes it quite challenging to read but also makes each poem an adventure in following the complex logic of the poetic "I." Of course, it also presents a serious problem for the translator, who must avoid filling in the ellipses in a bid to make the translation more accessible than the original.

Also typical in this poem is what is absent: any overt relationship with the tradition as well as any trace of humor. The latter is by no means surprising. Russian poetry has traditionally taken itself very seriously, and in this Polonskaya is in no way an exception. The former, however, is quite unusual. After all, as my colleague Ilya Kutik has put it, Russian poetry is a "citational epic" in which each poet tends to build by referring liberally to his or her predecessors. There are, of course, exceptions to this rule, and Polonskaya is one of them.

Finally, this poem displays one other feature of her narrative technique: an almost Chekhovian tendency to use the final line or lines of the poem to provide unexpected but extremely effective closure. Here it is in the introduction of the parishioners, who register the voice's presence even as we recognize that their own mortality has been prefigured in the sound that is doomed to die away. We see a similar technique, for example, at the end of the first poem in the "Portraits" section, "The Monk and the Child." That narrative, which focuses on the plight of a poor monk in the provinces (Polonskaya manages to capture the desolate and hopeless feeling of provincial Russia with more clarity than any poet of recent memory), ends with the riveting and disturbing image of the abandoned child, who takes on uncannily adult traits, staring at the monk "out of the corner of his eye."

Although all the poems in this collection are lyrics, and Polonskaya has never written any poem longer than a page, many of her poems nevertheless have an epic quality to them. This is true even in some of her elegies. A fine example is the poem "Saga," which I have chosen to begin the section entitled "Elegies."

Ages passed before our time: heretics blazed on pyres,
balsam wafted through rooms, shop counters
stank of gutted fish and of shirts' salty sweat.
Even then the moon was sugary, as if the closed blinds
in stifling silken rooms had squeezed a slice of lemon.
Inside were portraits and screens, and the moist gray walls
had eyes, like people. What do I care! Children
took over from exhausted women, and so it went, until . . .

We suddenly discovered the sun, and we were vouchsafed white stones
and a dusky and wild body. You had to take it
to elicit groans with your blows. You took it, removed it from the world,
but a gray cooing dove was able to cross the ocean.
Someday a woman's hands will send me glass planes,
cubes wrapped in chains, where your head will float
in a bitter brew steeped with oak bark and basil . . .

Fools! If you believe, then believe—you'll have time till you reach heaven
to recall the happy hours you spent
gossiping with neighbors over a cup of mocha
while I, in the midst of a warm valley between two lonely hills,
tended and caressed that sleeping profile, asleep like a tired nomad.

This poem provides both a series of striking images and a story. From the very title, of course, we can expect a story, but this is no saga in any conventional sense of the word. It begins with an evocation of history, but the history evoked is more of the "one damned thing after another" type than any specific nation's story. The love story that forms the basis of the elegy begins only in the second stanza as a sudden eruption, a clear break with the endless repetitions of the first stanza into a new kind of historical time in which events are apparently unique. For whatever reason, however, the narrator's ahistorical happiness cannot last, and now she expects to receive her lover's head, presumably severed from his body for having preferred history to domesticity. The final stanza returns to the narrator, who recalls her own lost paradise, figured again in the head of the beloved, that same lost head that can return only after it has been violently removed from its body.

The themes of death, desolation, and mutilation, so prevalent in all of Polonskaya's poetry, come together most forcefully in her war poems. Though not directly alluding to the bloody conflict taking place today between Russians and Chechens, her military poems seem to be influenced by her political views. Perhaps the strongest of these poems is the one that begins the section "Times, Places, Moods" entitled "A Bar, Soldiers, and Death." In its grotesque and powerful evocation of conflict filtered through a vision of a bar's interior just outside the battle zone, this poem is almost Goyaesque. Within the poem, the conflict is between a song, which is traditionally a symbol of hope, and Death herself. The two are fighting for the life of the soldier, who sleeps unknowingly, his head on the bar. The final quatrain is horrifying in its simplicity and in its implied future violence.

> Toward dawn, when things quiet down, the song flutters up to a branch.
> Death, however, wakes up even earlier and gets there first.
> Having donned a linen shroud over her tattered clothes,
> she waits by the door, patient and ashamed, like a nurse.

I have chosen to close the collection with a poem that forms a bookend with "A Voice." "The Gale" presents the tautest and most terrifying of all of Polonskaya's miniature narratives.

> 00.15 Water in the hold. The deck rocks.
> We sail. A taut wire of legs,
> we bespatter the walls.
>
> 00.45 We're sinking. The anchor glows
> like a farewell star. Wind rasps, the crew cries,
> the sea sucks the Great Bear.
>
> 00.53 The storm laid the blueness of its hands
> on the heeling boat. Called for help,
> no answer. Nothing lasts forever.

From a sinking ship, a voice is released. There is no response, and all hands, presumably, go down with the ship. What remains is the trace of the voice in the form of a poem, perhaps the only thing that remains after us "today or tomorrow."

Andrew Wachtel
Evanston, Illinois

A VOICE

A Voice

A voice bouncing off boarded-up windows, a quivering voice
within walls like well-driven nails.
A throaty voice, as of a caged dove,
groping through deaf darkness into bunches of hanging fingers.

Through them, through the air heated by snow,
torn apart like fabric, like flesh that has known the scalpel.
How silent it is! Either a hot flash on the cheek
or simply snowflakes melting and rolling down like tears.

That voice! Free, unmaimed by wheels, not pursued,
edgy, floating beneath the damp stone vaults,
remarked only by the lightning glances of parishioners
who will remain in this blue twilight, today or tomorrow.

Portraits

The Monk and the Child

In the cognac twilight sheep hearts will keep on beating to the
    rhythm of the switch,
after our exile a stocking's elastic will slip down—air ripped by
    shepherd's smoke;
returning home, by the church doors a monk will find his sorrow
    in a reed basket—
an abandoned child, whose age
will suggest beating a path to the silted pond; but having torn
    away
the yellow rushes with his nails, he'll draw back from the water in
    terror,
having seen the wrinkled white triangle
of a face and not his star
in the reflection. Loud steers will bellow in the stockyard.
And then, having emptied his backpack, he'll stomp
cheese and blood sausage into the roadside dust and roll in
    wormwood until dawn.
He'll go mad and lose his faith in the spines of wise books,
in joyful blackberry fields, and in the vaults
where once he mortified his flesh and repented with lowered eyes,
    but only in Latin;
the child will sleep tranquilly as children do, and upon waking
will stare at him—out of the corner of his eye.

OCTOBER 12, 2000

The flower girl

entered the florist's shop where the funny little parakeet pecked
   her hand.
Now he's sick—combed up his coif with a fading feather.
The sunset sank stickily into the canal, grabbing blindly at the buoy;
stacking sacks of cargo, truckers laughed on the nearby tracks.

But the woman remained alone in her fast-fleeting years.
Awoke to an empty bed, an oily mattress.
Liars and lie abouts nuzzled wives in their happy homes
before breakfast, draping their flabby bodies astride.

Their problem. Raw life looks dull out the window.
You get used to ignoring it.

Slowly, she watered her plants
and thought: I'm not as old as they say, but if you listen to
   vulgarity . . .
Chucking his things around that feller acted like a bank teller.
It's OK, but it seems my time has passed.

By midday the parakeet seemed asleep, another lie.
Lunch break. Key in the back pocket, and wrap the bird in
   newspaper.
By the time you open it up, it ain't worth reading; what the hell,
let's walk along the riverbank—used to be a lot of bums

around here. Why, why have all the willows been chopped down?
The canal, like a cancer patient, filled with oil like some drug,
   displayed monster fish
yawning under awnings—awesome.
But folks are happy; they cry only to themselves.

Who'll get her flowers? Who cares?
Time to order tea from the bored waitress in the white apron.
Her feet blistered by new shoes: isn't it amazing how damp
this chunk of the blind homeland is? Never noticed that before.

She walked by the store, not looking back at the alley filled
with leftovers from former days, old ladies combing out rumors,
acquaintances from her block who'd grown up
into "big cheeses." Her excuse, paleness, exhaustion.

When she reached her landing
she bent over and looked down several times through the
    wrought-iron grate,
then entered the apartment (I can't see her).
With the point of a knife she stuffed a piece of paper under the
    steel door,
covered the opening, and turned on the gas.
Made the morning edition. She'd always wanted to be in the papers.

AUGUST 12, 2000

To Mama

I brush pine needles of sleep from your cheek in the mist
where the guards, wrinkling their tanned foreheads, warmed the
    roof with their curses.
In the nervous tannic air a fluttering swarm of butterflies,
and peonies, which die dripping blood, hiding from the shears in
    the bushes.

Your hands, hands like dry maple leaves, hidden in the amber
of a yellow room sappy with fresh-cut wood, how they burn!
Unknown time flows through the ailing window frame,
and crows stick their nests like birthmarks among the branches.

The flannel of space dries on a line, changing color,
baked by the summer, bread cools, sweets lose their flavor.
Clouds, random pieces of upside-down china, bang into the rafters,
and pine columns thrust toward the sky, like a baleen corset.

2000

When she touched

his face her fingers ached, as if she'd dipped them in ice water.
In her memory only shards remained.
Better cast off, but there aren't any boats on the quay,
so you sit and watch marmalade birds freeze.

White. Very white, like that closeness, like the brightness of autumn
amid the maples, the rocks, and the sand flecked with gray.
"Hands off! Don't touch me," she'd said.
But that face tracked her everywhere, across borders even.

And from then on the cities—with jutting chimneys,
wet sidewalks, and soot-covered windows—
watched as she hunted everywhere: for the lashes, lips, eyes
which she'd begged—just don't touch me.

DECEMBER 27, 1999

Novitiates

In the sticks novitiates get to know labor and wear kerchiefs,
lonely lights glow, currant bushes bend to the ground by the
    roadside,
the skin of maiden cheeks is untouched.
In the morning cocks crow and fog blankets the houses.

But when can you think about all this? While undressing,
    smoothing the sheets?
Between the extinguished light and sleep there's but an instant;
olive night pours through the rectangular window,
and the whisper of lips, afraid to touch.

JUNE 23, 2000

■ □ ■

I wake up and drink in the water's transparent fabric.
My head's bent sideways like a barley stalk,
the hem of my skirt is rumpled, the windows gape
like dry mouths ready to suck in and spit out the cosmos

into my bed; please, where can I run?
The chair looks dead, like a tortured tortoise,
feet sticking up in the air, a dagger in the heart;
I read about the executioner's block that killed a king,

a king whose people mocked him for words
that would later become soiled by overuse.
But then, exhaling stench, they cried out: "Rise up!"
His scarlet silks were ripped by iron.

JULY 2000

Eyes

Step toward the window—your eyes are dead,
for they've been dipped into and greedily drunk out of.
Your eyes are like a sandbar, like burnt-out steppe pastures,
so step forward at last and bring others close with a gesture.

Let them remember what it means to live without turning on a light,
without recognizing shadows at noon
or dipping their faces into a bloody dawn. But no,
they fell back when you came,

for it was not you, no. It was I—just a rumor.
Listen to hearts breaking: from the black maw
I blindly rip out two more
exhausted ones, but if only crazy

passion had eyes and could see!
So that above the eyelashes, above the heads, above and alongside . . .
Your dead glance has frozen, and up ahead is barefoot
girlish night and a flat field, calm as a glassy sea.

Outlines of a Portrait

1

After sunset shadows take on another aspect.
In the cup of a man who personifies indifference
to everything, even to his shirt color,
clear soup congeals into aspic.

His collar's unpressed,
stained with ink or fingerprints perhaps.
Moths fly out into the world
from the corner of a rolled-up mattress.

2

He looks out from God knows what age
(one can only guess what happened to his eyes).
He switched flags and ran, stood on the deck of a sinking boat,
caught a taxi with flooded brakes.

He found the moon in a quatrain's company,
on the polished surface of a scratched desk,
recalled the city where he was "superfluous,"
from his swollen facial nerves to his old-fashioned pants.

He well knew that his back hid a whip's sign,
his jacket—his bearing, as he stood endlessly at the docks
where fishermen's nets billowed, smelling of iodine.
And on the market square a woman's voice called out dully
to a disappearing ghost, to the ghost of a maritime storm:
"Salvatore! Salvatore!"

Calculator

You get up, move about, bang into the room's corners.
A way off, a mournful-sounding horseshoe clomps,
crossing the asphalt road.
It means there are still horses.

In the twilight of difficult winter motions,
with a clod stuck to the brown leather
of a boot, patched and worn by your devotions,
you divine the sun as a favor

to the hills, farmers, plowed-up pastures.
Completely unnoticed you rush out.
The drawn-out air cuts your breath like cord
as you pass the slanting nameless block.

Like an ashy fly, a cloud of soot
crawls from ear to ear across the scars
of high-cheekboned airplane heights,
where there's a calculator lacking calculation

fixed by a careless hand.
You look ahead, up ahead is fate.

Sky

He broke up the sky on the square and gave it like breadcrumbs to
    birds.
Then he cut it into pieces and threw it to the beggars,
the crazies, the blind, and their companions.
But I got an end, smashed like a cup thrown to the ground,

lying on its back like a wounded soldier,
uncomplaining, as a harem wife
hiding her gaze behind a black veil.
The plains' bed is spread with houses, and everyone

beneath it ages like a slave chained in bondage,
save his high-cheekboned face.
Tensing my voice I started to refuse my free portion.
But I stayed mute; the sky's mouth was filled with lead.

JANUARY 5, 2000

Image

The night's squeezed out. On the red cornea of the windows,
the bumblebee of dawn.
The aging lips are sucked in like a whirlpool
and they disturb the air like a blacksmith's bellows.

This is how a mother's image fades.

And the daughter stands by the iron knobs
keeping the child from the transparent lids,
from the brows sharp as blades;
a ripe olive branch
on a medallion clutched in balled-up fingers.

Then suddenly the priest enters soundlessly.
The child wriggles vigorously in her arms.
He runs away, pressing himself to the cook; it smells of plums,
the worn cotton of the apron rips along the seam,

and the medallion drops from gaping fingers.

APRIL 20, 2000

Salvatore

Night forced the Milky Way through a pin—the sirocco
ruffles dogs' manes on the buckwheat beach;
fish have their own Auschwitz—in nets and boats;
two fishermen doze in a taverna, a third's at sea.

Lambswool waves dry out on dead reefs;
on the walls a tower of shadow, like spiders round the neck;
the wet nurse is correct, the child obedient,
and the world has closed its eyes as if there are no executioners or
    victims.

Good news awaits Salvatore on his journey;
his spouse successfully starched the lace dress;
the storm skirted the quick pirogues,
and the white star lies like a woman embraced.

APRIL 30, 2002
MALDIVES

Refugees

The procession arrived one Sunday morning,
white as a miller; children choked on sobs,
women smoked, carelessly curling their lips:
I understood that you're the governor no longer.
Leaning a tear-stained cheek against the wall
you gazed at them, horribly maimed:
they lay between city and steppe
on boards lashed together, all cheekbones and clenched teeth.
They lay, boots dusted with topsoil,
having failed to find memory,
like so many scrolls pulled from someone's breast pocket,
no use to God or Patria.
By the lakes, as on the Kremlin towers,
the shadow clock showed noon.
And people fell, and people lay
like grain in a fresh-plowed field.
Having crossed the road the fog knifed through
like a logger in a virgin forest.
And in your eyes I saw despair
and I feared to look into the prophet's eyes.

NOVEMBER 19, 2002

Elegies

Saga

Ages passed before our time: heretics blazed on pyres,
balsam wafted through rooms, shop counters
stank of gutted fish and of shirts' salty sweat.
Even then the moon was sugary, as if the closed blinds
in stifling silken rooms had squeezed a slice of lemon.
Inside were portraits and screens, and the moist gray walls
had eyes, like people. What do I care! Children
took over from exhausted women, and so it went, until . . .

We suddenly discovered the sun, and we were vouchsafed white
    stones
and a dusky and wild body. You had to take it
to elicit groans with your blows. You took it, removed it from the
    world,
but a gray cooing dove was able to cross the ocean.
Someday a woman's hands will send me glass planes,
cubes wrapped in chains, where your head will float
in a bitter brew steeped with oak bark and basil . . .

Fools! If you believe, then believe—you'll have time till you reach
    heaven
to recall the happy hours you spent
gossiping with neighbors over a cup of mocha
while I, in the midst of a warm valley between two lonely hills,
tended and caressed that sleeping profile, asleep like a tired nomad.

SEPTEMBER 15, 2000

Autumn Gulls in Prague

1

Gulls of my torment, gulls
with breasts pierced by the lances of gothic spires,
you're eaten alive by the rusty waters of wharves,
then the soot of dusk will blacken your worried wings.

2

Desolation. Bridges joined, an iguana's back
arched like a bony comb;
a three-pronged sycamore displays a yawning wound—
the fourth trunk amputated by lightning.

3

The wind's vassal throat
shudders, freezes in gulps.
I wrap myself in tomorrow's
ripe bitterness
which grows into glass, like shoots of sky,

in the river's dissolute ribbon—
the gulls' mussed-up feathers—
in the echo of trodden stairs,
in the fate of slippery cobblestones,

in the tough meat of trams
(wombs for their passengers).
Tomorrow we part.
The gulls fall silent. . . .

NOVEMBER II, 2000

Love Story

. . . I remained standing, my back to the ocean.
The vanishing city looked like an open vein;
squawking gulls swallowed fog,
their open beaks crying, "Write a novella about us!"

Seagulls, like the scratch of a damp hunter's match;
a shepherd brought me love on a platter—what could I do with it?
Those gulls, like eyebrows preserving duplicity,
are dying.
But I never wrote a novella.

FEBRUARY 14, 2000

Sea Song

That sweetness. That sweetness you left inside me. . . .
I'll ask the mountain gods, Will you show your faces?
Between a groan, my groan, and the heavens—a salt breeze,
in the silky valley a frightened herd of horses cantered off.

Apricot evenings and a mountain wreathed in blue mist.
Blind grief wanders the wet foothills, stumbling into corners.
At dusk, a woman scalding milk
will say that the youngest god, as if wielding a club, wounded the
    sea's breast with a star.

Iodine air, like sea blood, dolphins leaping from nets.
Toward morning the fisherman hauled a quivering cargo up from
    the depths.
The woman became silent, spilled the milk, and divided up some
    bread—
the rye taste broke through the sweetness you'd left behind.

APRIL 29, 2000

La Pasión

We hung a white flag from the house—the inquest is over.
We chewed dirt. With our fingers we crumbled up the glass goblets
from which we had just drunk liquid the color of blue vitriol,
and then we renounced each other. Eventually

the atmosphere became unbearably suffocating,
but to look away would have been to go blind.
One guest suddenly said: "God, how gorgeous!"
looking either at her or at the mounted

fish someone had placed under glass.
Those guests! Today they recognize you, tomorrow they won't
acknowledge your existence. But they'll club a gaffed fish,
repeating, "*La vida fatal. La vida.*"

NOVEMBER 16, 1999

To E.P.

Distant vistas pregnant with rain
and I swallow twilight-tinted air—don't weep!
Our garden's like a wounded beast.
Don't go there. I'll pick roses to close his eyes with; give
me a storm's power and the balance of a little boat filled with people,
but don't open the door.

Someday—only please, don't weep,
we won't be able to stay together. . . . Most likely
I'll remain to wander among the pines. I'll love you
as I remember you; for now, give me half
of that love—to guard the milky morning birds and the early dawns
until I harden like sap.

■ □ ■

I wake. A room, narrowed by radiators,
its transom window just a farce.
Rays have nothing in common with snakes
but they force you to the window to look at Mars.

Forty-odd years of glory or rut,
plus those lying already in the ocean depths. . . .
Others will turn your house into a ruin,
thinking with a smirk about the coming day.

In the orchard apple trees will still grow,
a child will run and pull his mother's hands,
recalling his father, at least in his glance,
if a glance can really recall anything.

You alone will lose color and voice, change faiths.
In the fiery beams of a lighthouse, passing ships
will sooner discern the unfriendly gray shore
than your profile, so far from the round earth.

A Dream

To the memory of B. . . .

The traitorous color of mica in apertures of yellow,
on the windowsill the wrong flowers,
and the smell of ground pepper instead of tobacco.
A shaking hand with a cigarette
mixed up a portion of cake,
and the woman smoked seriously.

The smoke deepened her exhaustion,
searching out the cataract of nighttime emptiness,
and the cat-patterned curtains flapped
as always.—Years had passed.

Strangers were happy to shuffle their slippers,
the poor little girl found another place.
Corners—four silent male nurses,
fences, eternity—stuffed
into forty square feet.

■ □ ■

The telephone's silent, as if murdered.
There's no war on but they're asking me to surrender.
I'm sure I could run uninjured
through the bullets, but I wouldn't get any aid.

But what's actually happening to me is a bit different—
I'm growing from the earth, dawn's blood pours over my head.
I've been many things in this life: a fish pulled unwillingly from the
    sea,
a tree, a wind gust . . . but I've never yet been trampled grass.

DECEMBER 1999

I climb out the window across the street.
The walls' revenge,
the yellowish mouth
of someone else's stained window ledge.
Shadows hang down
glancing haughtily around.
Yesterday, at twelve-thirty,
my veins were sliced by the moon.
I wasn't the first,
I don't ask for glory or bread
as I glance calmly at the heavens,
remaining like a simple marcher in a parade.
But all the same, where were you
when I was carried
in someone's arms
right past your garden?

APRIL 16, 1998

I leave you a section of the doorjamb
from my Moscow apartment. Like the pawn that moves to
E-4 in the famous chess opening,
your body stiffened, it could not be sat at the table,
and it refused absolutely to serve
as a straight line's continuation,
like a fox trapped in its hole by a stupid spaniel. . . .
Where there is only emptiness between upper and lower lid,
where fear leads one to shut oneself up in an endless tunnel,
it is the same as waking up dying of thirst
and looking at the base of a pitcher,
guessing that it is where a worn-out tablecloth is hanging,
and groping for a long time on the wall
as if on a dolphin's smooth back.
You grope again, but you don't find the switch.

Love for a Man

Ringing like plangent bells.
Cathedral. Desert memories
mixed with the wet shine of hair.
The silence of sand. From today on
the days will steep, wrinkles will appear
on the forehead, as the roof of the mouth
accepts the gait of red wine on the rocks.
The cubes gathered first, then led me
to the guide. Chalk-white insteps
commanded us to lie down and
our white faces touched. Await an answer
in rays. In expectation of full possession
the trivial wounds were cauterized.
Our hearts crashed against jetties,
jumped like cats in a junkyard.
The guide led the blind along—
it hurt them to face the dawn.

I Frequently Dream of America . . .

I Frequently Dream of America,
dryness in the throat,
from private properties.
A swelling—the reddish tiles of a roof,
America, Russia's inside-out opposite, breathes.
Over there. That's why I can't sleep here.
Whose idea was it to make poets?
Watch a carp die for a fancy banquet.
Beg for money at the local bank.
Replant an uprooted aspen,
head off to Chicago, fly to Aspen.
The result: a garbage can.
The explanation: Russian or not.
Sea slugs, swarms of spiders,
poetry juries in the corridors.
It's getting light. Cinderella changes.
Wandering spring hammers nails
remaining indifferent to everything.
I Frequently Dream of America.

The Postman

The doorbell. The postman squirming in the corridor.
I fear news, telegrams, announcements,
blue or yellowish forms,
and bags swollen like a knee swathed in bandages
slung over the shoulder.
I hear "Sign here," but the signature smudges
in the middle, because ink is also a mistake.
The postman opposite me. A smile
melts over his face, covering up treachery.
Could it really be a fear of night fog,
or of wind trapped in the drainpipes?
Could it really be memories of you? . . .
"Good-bye" and your heels crunching on the snow.
The night of a vanishing era
reads an unknown telephone number.
But perhaps there was no postman?

The Polish Woman

A swallow burst into the hardening shell of sleep.
Rain whacked the glass like an officer whipping his orderly.
A multistemmed lilac scattered flowery rust,
and the sky covered the hills like a quilt.

A slice of tram blades, a shoe's soaked felt.
The river foamed, harking to the steeples' splinters.
And a marble angel, unable to utter a sound,
froze in the uselessness of her wings.

How the pharmacist frightened you, clicking the shutters closed!
Turn around, become the token of asphalt streets
with incomprehensible names where cast-iron old age lives,
where slaps are an everyday morning affair.

But whenever the coal cooled in your house's hearth
after so many days of forgetting *her,* after . . .
Touching the switch, you'd remember the rag's edge
and the eyes, the inconsolably moist eyes of that Polish woman.

MAY 21, 2001

To . . .

Oh, those endless months in the sticks!
Just black derricks of stationary firs,
just shouts in courtyards and birds' wings
scraped into bonfires by a hunchbacked hunter
by the tattered delta.
You come upon things you don't want to find:
crumpled blouses from suburbs,
garbage in dives and entryway tiles
painted a dirty green,
an adolescent's swoon.
How happy the walls are, guarding the innocence of others
that they can't see!

I know you like the earth, with all my body,
I know you with all my body, like hunger. . . .
Come to your senses, let me control my voice!
You seep away drop by drop, like youth, by the drop,
like blood in a sticky bandage.
Buying up tickets in overheated booths
to antique girls and boring free verses;
electricity burns in copper cocoons,
perfume permeates heavy elevators,
and cabanas, gone feral in winter, are waiting.
But I remain with other people's deaths,
in the autumn ochre, in a sworn lie
(autumn's like faces here), and a soldier pleads:
"Lady, give me money for cigs"—a soldier in a tight uniform.

Oh, these endless months—like shards of cold;
and our souls, like plowed-up fields;
not like a fishy cold, but like hoarse exhaustion,
and like yesterday's unrepeatable day;
thus are our days short.

JUNE 2002

Scherzo

As peasant pitchforks raked hay into stacks of lilac night
and reflections of signs danced in bronze sheet metal ponds,
you dropped needles of pine eyelashes into the palms of another
    woman,
and the floorboards, fearing to give us away, seemed like chalk . . .

. . . so light a candle to those days, to the finches for their silence in
    clay,
for souls that are sometimes harder than tin plate.
A quick-moving speedboat cutting screwlike through the waves,
that is the face of vengeance.

MARCH 11, 2001

Times, Places, Moods

A Bar, Soldiers, and Death

Like chained dogs, the gravel piles of vigilant mountains guard the
    bay.
The cold keeps concealing its face beneath a fan, tender and rosy,
while the sun, powerless to do anything, hides and bites its lips;
the clinking walls of fat mugs resound in the barroom; the wind
    blows and blows. . . .

Inside, what with the stomping combat boots, it is inaudible of
    course.
A song—hair and combs dance in curlicues of smoke;
stars, hanging down from the roof like children, peer into the
    windows;
dresses, chevrons, cuffs, the dresses peppered with rose corsages.

Stems in glass vases, beads of sweat beneath brows,
glances—dagger blades; a beery floor, steamy air;
tomorrow the road . . . paved with rock,
edged with gnarled burls of trees, souls pinned to that road.

Adam's apples in front; gulping the burning strong stuff.
Far from the twisted lumpy trenches, the earth hut—
gaping like the suddenly opened cage of a feral animal,
fed and caressed with the warm palms of life—

far from the whistle of shells, the drawn-out hissing of shrapnel,
far from the swollen unshaved cheeks of a sand-strewn face
crawling around somewhere nearby, frozen in horror a yard away,
with its livid eyes, the eyes of a victim.

Far away, in a nasty dive filled with laughter and women's shouts,
he dreams, hurriedly plopping his head on the wooden bar,

settled into his skin, a net of wrinkles and cracks.
His catnaps are shredded, like this war of the pitiless.

Toward dawn, when things quiet down, the song flutters up to a
 branch.
Death, however, wakes up even earlier and gets there first.
Having donned a linen shroud over her tattered clothes,
she waits by the door, patient and ashamed, like a nurse.

FEBRUARY 2, 2000

Caucasian Saga

Caucasus

It's December, one really must believe the calendar.
A couplet ripped from the throat; in the dark
dogs bare their teeth, death licks up the south,
and sunset billows the skies like a warm quilt.
The orders today—line everyone up in the courtyard:
whoever's too old to fight or simply too callow.
The capital exudes sleep, in the moonlight
the Caucasus pulled three times at the lock.
"I'm nineteen," said the sergeant suddenly.
"I'm scared, guys," the echo resounded.
Fist clenched in insubordination to the mountain,
but the stone ego is silent.
In dreams the power of gloomy faces.
They are legion amidst the frozen trees.
The widows turned into black swans here
to peck the eyes of the living and the dead.
The sergeant relaxed, not seeing the gunports.

The Capital

Life raced along like russet Tverskoi Boulevard,
leaving its notches on the trees.
Having nosed open the door to his room
with her foot, she kissed the bishop's hands.
The enormous transport of winter rolled into Moscow.
Doves of snow sat on the roofs.
They shot pain like petards,
splattering like champagne on the official ornaments.
War seemed a fantasy—the tramcars
slid like a newly hatched perch under the water.

Canvas took the place of someone's house
but those were all other people's windows.
Readers, inured to death,
welcomed the letters of their horoscopes.
Epaulets, moving their armchairs toward power,
were raping girls in trenches
and medics tried to gather up the tesserae.

Caucasus

Sergeant, sergeant, it's long since you slept!
Night descended along the alpinist's chokers,
the invisible threaded the peaks of cliffs
measuring a sharp necklace for the sky.
Battle cries faded over the dried-up stream.
A flashlight shined and faded out; someone
pulled hard at the sergeant's shoulder
as if trying to shake out his soul.

■

He remembered nothing but the eyes and lips.

NOVEMBER 2002

The Provinces

Bloody mallards; a wispy fog on the swamp;
his son preferred the company of quiet women
with filthy glances; the local priest smells more of the body
than of humility—that is what the pearly white teeth and the
    curtains whispered.

The people, black as moles, scattered, became one with the night.
Later in a peasant hut they take an infant from a woman with
    their dirty hands.
Bast sheets, faces sweaty from the harvest,
a heart hidden under a faded blanket:

What is it? A scar oozing blood into the sunset like a god
or simple gray clay mined from the bottom of a lake?
The poor priest. The book's pages are crumpled.
Days spent around the table evoke nothing but yawns.

JULY 16, 2000

Sunday

Sunday market. Stalls set out like crumpled tinfoil,
pigs' heads blinded by sudden death
groan in search of gutters, God observes.
My pockets are empty.
I lose you amidst the motley shopwindows, the salesmen's aprons
from raspberry to russet, flecked like the cheeks of an apple;
a melon's flesh like the body of a starfish,
counterweight anchors tossed on the scales.
A bell, torn by the ear from the distance (Where are you? Where is
    your hand?).
I'm stunned by the hypocritical foreheads, submissive to the
    church on Sunday.
Perhaps it's my nerves, perhaps the bare poplars like in Dachau. . . .
And by the roadside, spilled from a shopping bag,
some potatoes are strewn about.

SEPTEMBER 21, 2000

On the Riverbank

The honeyed leaves are tattered like a giraffe's skin on the plains;
canvas fishermen thread worms with coarse fingers;
the water has its own face; the sky, all in naked goose down,
floats over it like a lure, like a moistened bran bread ball.

The evening unloads coal as from a cart by the shovelful,
a wheezing radio pours out sounds of eternal music into waiting
    ears;
stars, like gnats stuck to a sugarloaf—starry horror
steals across a dead pike's dying eye.

OCTOBER 7, 2000

A night squashed like black currants—shadows frozen to earth;
a naked sea of maimed plaster statues;
a stray dog's eyes tear; look at the moon—a spider trapped in amber!
The emaciation of the exhausted forest horrifies, the maples die
   first.
A holy fool, his mouth sealed by hot ash,
grabs a goddess and tearing the flesh from her cheek with his nail
wraps her shoulders in rags the color of spent cartridges.

OCTOBER 17–19, 2000

Autumn

I feel for the heavily breathing, bluish flocks,
feel for the homespun, heavy-footed shepherds,
for the ivy-covered house with corner beams thrust rapierlike into
    the earth,
for love, which recedes on tiptoes

without looking back, gradually, until
the martens awake, curled up in the foliage;
paprika wafts from the kitchen; the sun sticks its horns
through the windows, a sure sign of fall.

That's how it goes; there's a boat but no oars,
just wait, our clenched fists are stronger;
and the seaweed tires of the sea it always drinks.
Come closer; the lines on your face look like sled tracks.

The Wasp

Bare trees, the shepherds' gear was packed and they themselves
    were gone.
No sound of hunting horn, no spaniel's bark.
All finished. We saw them off; it seemed they were still waving
from afar. But because of the snowstorm

I could answer only with a wink.
I went back in the house and poured some wine
into the ringing glass goblet, then stepped into
the floury dusk through which, it seemed, I heard

the strange but measured ticking of some hidden clock.
Wherever I went I heard it—it
was the buzzing of a belated wasp
practically in winter, practically in a snowstorm.

"Where in the world have you come from?" I asked the wasp.
Two filmy wings. You could have saved up summer
in a shepherd's pouch, but you found shelter
in my heated house. Somewhere,

perhaps from the waterlogged pipes, came the sound of jazz,
or perhaps the heavy trunk of some tree bent and
groaned—it was all far away from us.
We're in the apartment alone, and it will soon be Christmas.

DECEMBER 1, 1999

November 23, 2000

The snow, white like exhumed bones in a pit,
flies, flies into the eye's empty abyss;
anger held in check like a steel spring
spasmodic. . . .

A rope ladder for a blind man;
a bucket of water for a desert wanderer;
the sunset's presented like a ripped-out heart
and a pounding in the temples.

A draft hunches your back like a question mark;
the streetlight, an unwilling boutonniere,
throws light that looks like a ballerina
and a crow trapped in a bottle.

DECEMBER 2000

In winter the rooster's mute.
The camel hair blanket retains
and hides a head and body's shape.
Trees are alive, and the earth
rests under whiteness. Peerless.
Darkness comes early in winter, and one's sight
takes time to adjust, it appears.
A distorted passerby through the transom window,
back bent like a question mark.
A buzzing fly between the panes—an echo
from the past. He crossed himself off the list.
Aging's no subject for a detective.
Still, a hanging wrinkled raincoat
recalls eternal greatness and
the fact that two are gone. But the trace
of presence in the cup on the table
and on the stained wallpaper
remains, like a private eye in the library.

■ □ ■

In shelters of homeless December
a babbling garland of voices,
the drowsiness of a twilit block in the window.
In my broken-up soul, hanging on a pawnbroker's lock,
in exchange for the delirium of confessions
made up of our desires and caresses,
stands our love, stripped in punishment
on the square of half-open mouths and eyes.

Solitude

Ashy sky in my windows. Locked in the North.
It's slick on the bridge of solitude—you're not surrounded
by cobbles and stone but by eyes, the eyes of a grief-stricken hart,
a bloody drop in the left one.

Solitude! Like spittle on the lips of a cretin,
like flight, hiding in the bell-shaped cotton hem
of a mother's skirt in the street's calico carnival:
that is solitude in this world of appearances.

Like a brand-new exile in a well
in which standing water, sticky with algae,
turns into old ladies who refuse the horde's subjugation
and in whose soft centers needles fall monthly.

NOVEMBER 5, 2000

Islam

Having once quitted its citadel,
we can't do it again. How sublime your feral hands were!
What can doctors know about them?
What would a priest say about them while dunking a child in a
    font?
A soldier who holds weapons above all?
But in the ramshackle hut where a Bessarabian fixed my shoes

he answered me: "Leave everything as it is.
To the servant myrtle and incense,
to the schooner gales and a strong mast, to pilgrims Mecca,
to war's losers futile revenge.
Let commanders exchange scars for laurels on the march.
But leave yourself the copper of an inkwell on your desk."

JUNE 18, 2001
ISTANBUL

Turkish Themes

Whites fill the black tunnel of pupils.
Barges settle scores here, having chosen the Bosporus.
The insatiable hunger of the sea that swallows rocks,
the bright green phosphorescence of a falling star

touched by a gull's wing and transformed into drops.

The ripped-out sinews of soft rag ladders.
The boat of ecstasy bobs, rubbing its tie-line.
Don't take away life with the telephone's bustle.
The horizon's spoiled the taste of the sea with an island.

I prefer a lie in the motley clothes of a gigolo.

JUNE 16, 2001

To S.Ch.

We sleep. Nailed to the beds,
to the iron frames and the ancient mattresses.
How painfully branches lash our eyelids as we sleep!
A bloody spot of roses is dying in the living room.

How hemmed in we are, divided
not by a guillotine or by a verbal sentence,
but willy-nilly, coal-black glances and a shared cell;
drop by drop, like two ruins, like salt water

we lie pressed against each other,
sharing an address:
on the roof's our stepson—a solid stork
with an iron heart and an open beak

stuck into the spongy pumice—
it's time for fogs.
We sleep, not sensing that life's too short
not to love, before we collapse into sand and ash.

MARCH 15, 2001

The Bell

The bell pierced the cloud skyscraper like a bat.
How it rang, deafening the poverty of the surrounding blocks!
A crowd was wheeling about by the door, holding little ones by
    the hands,
and the clawlike winds were flaying the birch bark off like skin.

And the embankment hurried to flip its glance upside down into
    the water,
as if it hadn't seen that beyond the gardenia a despot
had sprayed women, a cripple, and a thief with the slush of his eye
and had smiled at children.

APRIL 10, 2001

Missionaries

How silent it is, my Slav!
A caravan of Bactrian hills quivers in the south,
money-changer suns have devalued rubies,
and the evening, like a youth, lays hands on itself.

Philistine windows, crackling collars,
seal-black city-slicker eye shadow,
and a crush of people at the cinema entrance
like the stiff rings of cold Saturn.

Our general was hanged in September
by the town hall; books burn on fires
and plaster-eyed lions root in the ashes
and emaciated defrocked monks fall from the wharf.

The train shakes and limps in the ruts,
words hiss in Cyrillic like meat over coals,
dogs cough at doves in the willows,
our white standard's crushed by a crowd of streets.

O my patriarch! Death—a woman,
one for us all—is our prisoner, but if she's been treacherous
leave her. The night's black as a Moorish woman's skin,
sweet smelling as smoking incense.

MARCH 16, 2002

The Canvas City

A square where for centuries they chopped heads and built bonfires,
where holy men twisted their sparse beards,
how keen are the knives in your pockets!
Nothing there is shorter than life.

The city of canvas huts fell
like a laden camel, legs frozen into poles.
Wrapped in a rag, a dead child
stares through a hole at the stars.

2001

Song of the Fallen Heroes

Barrack-room cold, and sunsets that long ago turned into
    ptarmigans.
Overcoat sadness, gray, seemingly glued to our backs.
Rough stubble beards can't make our young faces mature.
Gravelly snow doesn't cool bare fingers down.

Moonlight behind us like an eye in death's shroud.
Breaking the salty sheen, garlands plunge into the sea.
Volleys of memory, like tears of faithful girls.
Hands of time blacken ruddy cheeks blasphemously.

Russet clay fields smooth out our lined foreheads.
Souls in revolt, we will strive to fix ourselves in bronze.
Nights will be tinged with our spilled blood.
It's a pity that dry wells can't resurrect the sun.

Morpheus of all the gods was our favorite.
Chests having flattened bullets, we march in formation into the
    future.
Who are we? Trophies taken by war from life.
But we're no longer here, and we won't return.

SEPTEMBER 9, 2001

Coda

The Gale

00.15 Water in the hold. The deck rocks.
We sail. A taut wire of legs,
we bespatter the walls.

00.45 We're sinking. The anchor glows
like a farewell star. Wind rasps, the crew cries,
the sea sucks the Great Bear.

00.53 The storm laid the blueness of its hands
on the heeling boat. Called for help,
no answer. Nothing lasts forever.

ABOUT THE AUTHOR

Anzhelina Polonskaya was born in 1969 in Malakhovka, a town thirty miles outside Moscow. Formerly an ice dancer in a traveling Russian troupe, she is the author of four collections in Russian: *A Voice, The Sky Through a Private's Eye, Poems,* and *My Heavenly Torch.* She lives in Malakhovka.

■ □ ■ □ ■

WRITINGS FROM AN UNBOUND EUROPE

For a complete list of titles, see the Writings from an Unbound Europe Web site at www.nupress.northwestern.edu/ue.